DESPATCHES HOME

WILLIAM NEILL

23 Livingstone Place Edinburgh EH9 1PD
Scotland
1972

Published with the support of
The Scottish Arts Council

SBN 903065 07 X

Cover illustration and design
by G. Gordon Wright

Printed in Scotland by
Macdonald Printers (Edinburgh) Limited
Edgefield Road, Loanhead, Midlothian

CONTENTS

ACKNOWLEDGMENTS
Some of these poems have already appeared
in Scotia, Catalyst, Gairm.

DESPATCHES HOME

At last we have them all well fooled, well tamed;
they use our baths and lard themselves with oil,
truss up their souls and bodies in the toga.

The squireens speak school-Latin and affect
misunderstanding of the kerns from their estates
(less slaves these than their masters
whom we have flattered into Roman ways).
Now, when our swords save them from their own kin
and mind plays traitor, there's no need for gyves.

Up in the hills, I grant you, there are those
whose hides are dun with peat-reek and who keep their arms
tough as our own with "Carry! Thrust! Recover! ",
who watch and watch, and hope that we grow weak.

Ungovernable these, growling in their own speech;
lean as the wolves they prowl their bracken dales,
dream vengeance as the bards sing round their fires.
They curse their former lords—lost to Catullus—
and snarl like tigers when we bay them up.

Holding for the most part, then, to the Pax Romana,
out from the hills some few
attempt their bloody mischief on dark nights.
These demons armoured in enamelled bronze
hate us as we hate them.

                    We both despise
the Latin-lisping traitors of the town.

THE MIXTURE AS BEFORE

There are mortar and pestle poets
who crunch up the rock of truth
into a fine soft powder;
they mix this with the oily medium
distilled from their own conceits.

Others suck up the dust of the particular
with their mental vacuum cleaners,
damp it with enthusiasm,
squeeze it into a ball;
they heave this at the hard head
of the unheeding philistine,
against which it breaks up
and returns to dust again.

OLD SALT

To start a journey is not always joyful,
yet most would sail again across uncharted seas.
Remember our former voyages, under warm suns,
the smell of salt and timber and all natural savours,
the welcoming smoke beneath the far horizon?
O for a fair wind to drive again
the prow through hissing water.

Not for the shining gold we cruise
these dangerous seas that smile and roar by turns.
We stretch the canvas, tune the strings of cordage,
learn to obey the order of our calling
because we would not have it otherwise.

We seek tomorrow's tidings in bannered clouds
whose tale is hid from those who do not sail.

CONQUEST

Why man, we saw Conquest come on in his shining metal,
with his bannerets flaunting their might in the blue air,
the thundering thundering on the ground as he topped the hill,
no mercy in the golden gleam of his false crosses.
But under the thews of our limbs the bones trembled and held.

In that sword summer we stood while the laverocks sang;
up through our fear the scent of the earth rose sweeter.
Shriven, we cast the lust of the world from our minds,
held to our arms that we knew must shiver and break
before that awful onset that roared its certainty,
bore down upon us, mockery pointing and death.

Squared off, we braced in sets like dancers in a ring,
with blood on our teeth stood to our last defences,
stood while the pikes shattered and, wonder of wonders, watched
as the giants floundered and screamed and their henchmen fled
    before us.

SIAMESE TWINS

Before the twilight of the first birdsong,
swimming through this warm darkness I can feel
the unison that leaves us in the waking day.

But you will drag me from all comfort, from all warmth,
as you dragged me from the cradle of our first creation.

At times when the eye is clear I can reach out
to verities beyond your sullied scope.

Yet soon you call me back to muddy appetite;
I share your clay and merge within your lusts.

I sometimes shout and sing that I'll be free;
you'll die and rot, release me from your chains.

But then you crow with glee and wag your finger,
say that when you go down you'll drag me off with you.

FHIR THA 'D SHEASAMH AIR MO LIC

The title is taken from the first line of the
epitaph on Duncan Ban MacIntyre's tomb in
Greyfriars: "Man who stands on my tomb . . ."

The skull that held the songs of climbing and descending
and those long swinging bones that encompassed herds
beneath this obelisk lie in a crumbling city
that cannot echo now the native voice.

In this kirk yard of the Grey Friars
the sweet singer's voice is stopped;
without shame, it seems, occasional compatriots
gape by an epitaph they cannot read.

Fair Duncan of the Songs,
in words and ways they do not understand
you remain uncorrupted.

HUNGOVER JANUARY

Another year lost, January comes and I
freeze in a cold that's like the Norseman's hell
viewing the city with a yellow eye.

Wellwishing over, now we are sane again
recovered from that old, Druidic spell
and wondering if the snow will turn to rain.

Back to the daily rule, to the controlled passion,
the quiet guarded nod that means: all's well
as long as number one can get his ration.

Perhaps when all the booze has left the blood
we'll take a better view than we can tell;
in springtime even the thistle grows a bud.

ISLAND

Austere on the grey curve of yon far ocean
the crags reach bleakly to the steely heaven;
only the wings that sail upon the silence
disturb the emptiness of sea and sky.

No desert is more unvisited than this dark peak;
all terror lies upon its ultimate seclusion.
Yet, if the vision is held until the mind be still
there is a calmness in that solitude.

Those who are schooled to contemplate such distances
dream in the stillness of these gliding wings;
they, seeing the summit in the night's last hour,
watch for the dawn to light the rock again.

IN MEMORIAM
ALASDAIR MAC MHAIGHSTIR ALASDAIR

Great Alasdair of Clan Donald, chief singer of the Scots,
there's many a song I'd make for a man like you.
For the sake of living Gaels you laid by your soul
and changed your kirk as others change their shirts.

Hiding in the hills from the hate of the plump red butcher,
raging with grief for the Gael and bitter with love of Scotland,
when the glutted ravens had gone and the shame lingered,
you wagged your songs at them round the Castle Rock.

Some shopkeeper saw the broadsword between the pages
and the hangman burned your books at the Mercat Cross.

Did you smile, *fhir mo chridh'*, at the breeze that bore
your blackened broken pages up and down the Canongate
as a Scottish snuff to tickle traitor noses?

Alasdair, better than a gift of horses
this burning of your books;
Our verses smoulder and choke
in the stale fires of their indifference.

* Nach nar dhuit fein mar thachair dhuit
O Albainn bhochd tha truagh,
gann làn an duirn de Ghaidhealaibh
fhàgail ri uchd-bhuailt'. . . .

* "Is it not shameful, what has happened to you, poor sad Scotland,
leaving a mere handful of Gaels in the breast of battle. . . ."
—From MacDonald's own poem of 1746.

MARY

Old riddles taunt our grief.
Why should a golden girl
from all our caring take herself out of life?
Why plant, so early, in her glowing flesh
these coloured seeds that purchase sleep and death?

What waste, a mind so quick
to depart so suddenly from us,
to turn away from our dull common sense,
wander a haunted wilderness on her own.

We can recall her, paused in a different peace,
following the mood of the page,
loving the land where it battled with the sea.

For all the calmness of her eyes, the quiet smile,
her death is an experience that for us
cannot be recollected in tranquillity.

PROGRESS

There was a time when each man of this broken townland
could carry his rhymes in his skull like berries in a bowl,
and the long rolling ranting runs of the treasured tales.

There was a time when any woman of the place,
after the shearing, would card and spin for the weaving,
or knit you a gansey while giving birth to twins.

With only a few stones and bunches of tufted heather
these men could build a house for you, so strong
no western gale could tear it.

The men of this townland, so very poor were they
that their minds boggled at the thought of two brass farthings.
They talked in grave voices of things they thought concerned
        them,
like ploughing and sowing and reaping and carting in,
like birth and life and death and after death;
and in social moments they passed round one clay pipe.

It took progress to break this townland,
to icepick the traditions out of brain and blood,
to spoil the bards and strip the guts from the stories,
to squeeze the knowledge from the women's fingers.
It took all the horsepower of the factory machines.

It took the whole of wide heaven
and millions of volts and decibels
to drown their voices out,
make them forget
the land and life and death and after death.

But, glory be to progress, we managed it at last.

CITIES OF THE PLAINS

It does not strike you that, some day,
a man may well be better
standing on a bare hill in the most bitter wind
than in your cities on this blackened plain.
Some day the truth may live beside you, in your head
naked of wine, of any spell of illusion
to brace your dream against a coming day.
To some waste, howling wilderness we may go again
from our most present fatness.

Now from the flinty rocks we have struck oil,
now we grow sleek on curds and wine and wheat;
we lack good counsel, all our power is gone.
Time blinds and comforts falsely those who claim to lead,
who brandish swords of lath in creeping darkness.

The greatest of our cities may yet become
crushed rocks scattered wantonly on a cold desert.
After the flames die and the bones of men
mingle their grains with the sand,
from the dumb concrete owls will hoot by night
and in flamescorched boardrooms only rats will squeak.

There is no board of directors, no union when the gates fall.

CROFTING PIPER

Because, at home, by turning a switch
he can hear the drip, drip, drip
of the Saxon natter-torture
twisting his mind out of a Gaelic compass,
in the evening under this falling sun,
free from the hoodies who try to drag his soul
towards their useless virtues,
MacCowal treads the machair by himself,
marks out the ground and doubles it again.

Now, in these dying days when all pride grows thin,
whisky cannot be had, gaugers are many and the money scarce.

Skilled fingers, heart and breath,
ivory, blackwood, leather:
the chanter sings to the drone's beat
hiharara hihorodo
rings out again the ancient Bells of Scone,
sobs for the Lost Children,
or bellows-blasts a rippling Flame of Wrath
to set Patrick squinting again.

Too Long, Too Long (we are by far) In This Condition.
The righteous look down their noses,
the baffled tourist grins,
as MacCowal bears the treasure of Boreraig
under his oxter, chinking out coins
of *siubhal, tuarluath, crunluath,*
crunluath breabach, crunluath a mach:
a kind of gold that in this sunken time
pays up the interest due on history's usury.

A GREY DAY IN THE GAIDHEALTACHD

Today the mist spills down into the grey daylight;
not Matthew Arnold's Celtic cotton wool,
but the real Mackay that pricks the face like dirk-points
creeps up the sleeve and down the back of the neck,
a western wetness that defies all fire,
that only whisky banishes.

The hardier tourists stand on the pavement's edge
like gulls marooned by storm;
old Glasgow women remembering the kindness of grandfathers
covered by the sad green turf of Tom na h-Aingeal;
exploring Cockneys chirping to keep their hearts up
in this outpost of Empire, this Caledonian Khyber;
a small thin man in a kilt like Joseph's jacket
asserts a doubtful descent from stern and steelhewed tacksmen.

I stand, lugubrious in the door of a tartan trasherie
watching the twin churches, firm as chosen champions,
cold-gabling one another before the Sabbath battle.

Home polished pebbles and rednosed Harrylauder corkscrews;
well, what did I expect? A risen Cuchullainn perhaps
birling a caman round his head, and his hair standing out like
    nails
with the warrior-flame around him like a halo
belting the secret Saturday-night half-bottles
out from behind the dikes? Or perhaps an elder
fou as a *faochag* and dancing the Righle Thulachain
or offering us a *balgam* straight from the bottle?

Too much to ask for perhaps,
now that we're all conditioned
to technicolour Cullodens, and a porridge advert or two.

VESSELS

Retired from his heroic navigations
his mighty galliasse of fifty oars
was heaved ashore to bear his memory.
Devouring time gnawed at each spar and plank
but still the shipwrights kept the vessel tight.

The sages, idle on the summer beach
discoursed about the ship:
some said, this is another keel,
not the same thwarts and strakes
as those that sailed to Crete.
The very essence, others cried aloud
of that same ship that held our hero king!

This fleshly vessel, every seven years
replaces all its substance;
the secret wrights and chandlers fit us out.
Pegs, frames and spars. We go through all the stages:
skiff-child, yacht-youth, stout merchantman,
and then the old beached barge too dry for barnacles
biding its time by a forgotten sea.

Is there some essence still that ties this hulk
to long lost timbers? In this frame preserved
some common thing a sage's eye can see?

A SONG OF LOST LOVE

From a Gaelic poem *circa* 1750, possibly
by James Shaw of Glengairn on Deeside

I hide no sound of my sorrow's burden
from who may care to know;
towards the high pass of yon eastern mountains
my longing glances go;
at evening's falling my sad heart bids me
towards Glenisla there,
where I might find yet the green eyed maiden
her of the red-gold hair.
Through the close fir-wood at the darkest midnight
I'd stumble for her sake,
or battle gladly the mountain torrent
did but my sweetheart wait.
Splendid the silks that I'd put around her,
her wrists I'd deck with lace,
and she would give me a pleated swordbelt
wrought by her own hand's grace.
Full is my heart for my own beloved
maid of the calm clear eyes;
long nights I lie in the dark and sleep not
and hear my spirit's sighs.
In fitful dreaming again I see her,
lass of the golden braids,
her cheeks aglow like the rowan's berry
her brows like arches made.
My being burns lest she wed that other
and I on Highland ground;
lusty my body, my skin unwrinkled
each thew and sinew sound.
Sweet was her voice when she bade me welcome
ripe were her lips and red,
O bonnie Anna, my kind and true one,
would that we two were wed.

She left me not for my lack of cattle:
coaxed by their lowland ways.
I plough no furrow, I sow no barley,
yet should her table grace
trout from the clear burn, the finest deers' flesh
the brown buck of the craig;
the wild grey geese of the western islands,
the white swan of the lake;
grouse from the moor and light-breasted blackcock
the capercailzie of the wood.
Though I should win lands beyond Lochaber,
the wealth that in them stood,
the Laigh o' Moray and Proud Dunedin,
the high hills above,
that whole wide kingdom I'd count a trifle
beside my heart's love.

TO A MAN OF MULL

I knew him at the end of his last summer.
He shared his food with me, I drank his dram.
He sang, and spoke a little of the past,
remembering the men who worked the granite.

Here, in this empty quarter,
the cradle of my kinsmen,
he shared his store and thought.
A king can do no more.

His house was Scotland,
his tongue the mark of Scots,
his hospitality and grace of speech
an echo of that pride which ought to be.

I might go back again,
perhaps to raise a cairn
beside his roofless house
beneath the battlements
of yon abandoned quarry.

I would not reach a hand
to lay one stone upon another
unless, within those walls again,
a man like him might live.

They could be joined again,
these fragments of Dalriada.

CHRISTOPHER MURRAY GRIEVE

Better by far, this bard, than we deserve.

How well he sees
that we ourselves have thrust our summer away,
have lost our vision of brightness on the lonely path.
A rage most just,
a grief most dignified
for what we have become.

The link of blood
in every thought he writes
continues Henrysoun in wit
Dunbar in irony;
captures the essence
of the Grecian Gael.

The blow of his contempt
the dunt of a blade's edge
on a border buffcoat:
his epic grace
the plash of oars
dropping from a birlinn's gunwale,
gracefully measuring a needful path
out through the teeming sea.

BATTLE HYMN

We are the learned young,
we, who know all.
No questions to ask,
no angels to fall.

Our fathers say they heard
clear battle-trumpets calling;
rode in bright cavalcades
to their vain brawling.

Yet all their many deaths
by fire and water
left us no legacy
but threatened slaughter.

The falsehood of their gods
we shall with courage prove;
their broken shards of lies,
we shall by faith remove.

We are the learned young
we, who know all,
no questions to ask
no angels to fall.

HIRAETH

Returned from exile he surveys the wreck
of this old city that he left behind;
shielded from history by the traveller's cheque
strolls from the Palace to the Castle Wynd.

Watches, amused, his wife buy tartan trash
eats in hotels where lack of bawbees barred;
here, where he entered up the petty cash
unlocks all coffers with a credit card.

Scotland, he says, is strictly for the birds;
he gives in tips more than his brother's wage,
but finds it difficult to put in words
an odd desire to share his brother's cage.

VERSES OF EXILE

From the Gaelic of John MacLean, 1787 - 1848

I'm all alone in this gloomy woodland,
my mind is troubled, I sing no song;
against all nature I took this place here
and native wit from my mind has gone.
I have no spirit to polish poems,
my will to start them is dulled by care;
I lose the Gaelic that was my custom
in yon far country over there.

I cannot muster my thoughts in order
though making songs was my great delight;
there's little joy comes to smoor my sadness
with no companion to ease my plight;
each night and day, in each task I turn to
the ache of memory grows more and more;
I left my dear land beside the ocean
and now no sea laps my dwelling's shore.

It is no wonder I should be grieving
behind these hills in a desert bare,
in this hard country of Barney's River
a few potatoes my only fare;
I must keep digging to win bare living
to hold these wild threatening woods at bay;
my strength alone serves till sons reach manhood
and I may fail long before that day.

The month of May and the first of summer,
my strength is drained by the blazing sun,
that wakes from winter the forest creatures
where they lay weakly in den and run;
the prowling bears rise from winter slumbers,
a roaming band that's a sore mischance;
the snouted fly with his store of poison
deals wounds unceasing from his sharpened lance.

He stabs my face with an eager malice
till with his venom my eyelids swell;
there's no escaping his burning juices
that gall my eye like a flame of hell;
I have not space to relate the boldness
of each foul crawler that seeks its prey;
like to the plagues that the Pharoah suffered,
my mean condition from day to day.

In this wide world there come many changes;
I little knew in that other land,
how fond my dreams at the time of leaving
that in due time I'd be rich and grand;
a turn I took that was not for profit,
a lying hope made me cross the sea.
This land of trees is no land of freedom,
no herd gives milk nor flock their wool for me.

This is a country that's hard and cruel,
they do not know it who journey still;
evil the yarns of the smooth-tongued coaxers
who brought us hither against our will;
yet if they profit it won't advance them,
may they not prosper despite their loot,
the cursèd wretches who drive out people
since first this Clearance was set afoot.

Strong is the promise that they will make you
this place's virtues they'll loudly boast;
your friends, they'll say, now grow rich and prosper
nor lack for those things that men want most.
They'll fill your ears with each lying rumour
to make you follow them where they will;
where they appear, few escape them safely,
fortunate they who evade them still.

Drovers of men who come to seek you
will seal their bargain with a lie,
no single word of the truth they're telling
for what their tongues say, their hearts deny;
loud is their boasting of what this land holds
each thing that's rarest, waits to be won,
but when you come here, little you'll see then
but great tall forests that steal the sun.

When comes the winter, a bitter season
the forest branches are clothed in snow,
and no plain cloth is defence against it,
thigh deep and thick on the ground below;
but clouted moccasins and double stockings
and leather thongs are our forest boots;
rawhide and fur are our latest fashions
ripped from the backs of the forest brutes.

Without true learning and skill in dressing
I would be frozen from brow to chin,
the stinging winds of the freezing northland
kill feet and hands did I let them in;
a frightful cold takes the edge from axes,
the bite of frost blunts the hardest blade;
no smith or forge here to heal spoiled metal
so fire must melt ere one notch be made.

Great were the tales that they told in Scotland
their falsehood proved by our sorry lot;
I've never handled a silver dollar
although I'm told that they can be got.
A deal is made, but there's no coin passes,
though you have bargained that cash be paid,
they'll take your gear but they'll pay no money,
for flour and butter is all their trade.

I see no market, I see no fair day,
no wealthy drovers of cattle here,
nought in our townland but want and shortage
that can't be bettered for lack of gear.
No cause of envy, our sorry debtors
whose trifling treasures don't match the score,
head hung in shame and a debtors' prison
when they have rouped all the meagre store.

Before the case ever reaches courtroom
be sure the roup will increase the debt;
the law they get from the jury's handling
makes sure the reiving's not over yet;
through our poor country the sheriff travels,
by the court's warrant he hounds the poor;
I live in fear that I'll see him bringing
his debtor's summons towards my door.

I cannot say in these simple verses,
no skill have I in such words as tell
to distant friends all the thoughts that fill me
of yon dear land where I used to dwell.
But let who read this heed well its meaning
and give no ear to the liars there
who boast this land only but to hook you
and trim their profits from your passage fare.

Though I've been diligent in the writing
it's taken me a full month or more
to set to rights all the things I'm thinking,
to shape in words all that grieves me sore;
in my soul's depth such a sadness fills me,
each weary day adds its hours of strife,
no joyful song fills this forest prison
that holds me fast for what's left of life.

How changed my custom from my youth's gladness,
the sounding days round each merry board;
joyful my heart in each happy meeting
our days a-flying while our spirits soared;
now since I left you my heart beats sadly:
the hot salt tears on my cheeks were shed,
on Thursday last as I saw the packet,
her head turned eastward and her canvas spread.

EXODUS

Now they have prisoned us in screaming towns
our young go mad like rats in shrinking cages,
knowing their lives fall to an empty waiting,
a barren striving for their Friday wages.

The robber barons come to their own again
heich on the Hielants, laigh upo the Tay;
the wrinkled lip, the sneer of cold command
have driven the former henchman far away.

This place is emptier than a traitor's heart;
there's one square mile at least to every grouse.
Here, people pray, when the last child leaves home,
some alien technocrap will buy the house.

THE BALLAD OF CONDULLIE RANKINE

(A Sad but True Tale)

Condullie Rankine gaed tae war
at the battle o Shirramuir, man,
tae fecht there for MacLean an' Mar
wi claymore straucht an sure, man.
Condullie wis a piper bauld,
skeelie on drone an chanter,
but aye in Mull the tale is tauld
aboot his sair mishanter.

Like ilka piper o his day
a weel-kent *duine-uasal,*
he played (but no the Sabbath day)
ceòl-mór in Duart Castle;
't wis needful when he'd gie a tune
tae haud the pipes tae play them,
but wi him cam a rid-haired loon
whase task wis tae convey them.

Condullie piped the Clan MacLean
oot owre the hills an heather,
an played "Auld Stewart's back again"
for twinty miles thegither;
aye swankan et his heels in glee
the fernie-ticklit callant
whase conduct on that day maun be
the subject o this ballant.

They cam doun tae the lawlan plain
wi *caismeachd* soondan shrilly;
Condullie eased the bagpipes' wame
an gied them tae his gillie;
syne gowpit doun a braith or twa
drew forth his blade for battle
an sprang wi *"Clann 'illeathan gu brath"*
intil the muskets' rattle.

Then cam a muckle cannon-roar
Auld Nick himsel wad deave, sir,
and Rid-heid wisna lang afore
he thocht it time tae leave, sir;
he didna leave the bagpipes there
(the better for oor story)
but bare them fra yon sad affair
full pelt tae Tobermory.

Condullie birled his michtie blade,
dealt oot his dunts richt sairlie,
till aa at ance his chieftain bade
him soond retreat oot fairlie.
Condullie ran tae pipe the tune
tae whaur he'd left—weel gairdit—
his pipes, an fand yon rid-haired loon,
wi instrument, depairtit.

Condullie sware baith loud an strang
yon *balach* fain he'd flype, sir:
the road tae Mull wis dreich an lang
wantan the merrie pipe, sir.
Doun their lang nebs the tacksmen glared,
the chief sulked in his tartans;
Condullie, silent, hameward fared
wi lugs as rid as partans.

A wicked bard there wis in Coll
eke o the Clan MacLean, sir,
wha socht tae pour his share o gall
on puir Condullie's name, sir;
he hated chanter, drone an bag,
detested those that played them,
an when he heard the pipers brag
wi Gaelic sherp he flayed them.

"What think ye o the pipes, *a ghraidh*,
o great Condullie Rankine?
In battle when he laid them by
straucht hamewards they cam spankin,
streikt oot their drones like airms an legs
an swiftly fled disaster,
loupt on a lubber loonie's back
tae get them hame the faster."

Nou, aa ye wha wad pipe a tune
in *ceilidhs* or in battles,
ne'er trust a thowless, plooky loon
tae mind yir pipes an chattels;
when ye gae aff tae tak a dram—
in this ye maunna swither—
tak baith the pipes an loon alang
an hae yir dram thegither.

TILLEADH

Is cuimhne leam
an deidh nan laithean fada fiadhaich air sàile,
Machair uaine Srathchluaidh
sìnte fo bheannachd 'na greine
'sna beanntan uasal oirdheirc Earraghaidheil.

Am fear nach deachaidh riamh thar chuan
cha tig 'na fhradhairc an sealladh ud as boidhche:
tonnan a' pogadh traighean geal' a dhùthcha,
faoileagan a' sgreadadh gu h-àrd mu'n caladh
a b'aithne dha 's e og,
's an ceò ag eirigh bho teintean aoidheil a dhaoine.

RETURNING

I remember
after the long wild days at sea,
the green machair of Strathclyde
stretched under the blessing of the sun,
and the noble splendid mountains of Argyle.

The man who has never crossed the sea
will never have that most beautiful sight come into his vision,
the waves kissing the white beaches of his homeland
gulls screaming loud over a harbour that he knew when young
and the smoke rising from the hospitable fires of his kinsmen.

BAN-TRAILLEAN AN TAURIS

Eun a sheinneas cumha
measg sgeirean na mara
amhran is aithne dhuinn
a thuigeas do shìor-ghairm
a chruitein, an deidh do chéile.

Mise, mar eun gun sgiath
ni mi tuireadh còmhla riut,
is mi gu tur fo bhròn
fada bho dhachaidh nan Gaidheil.

Boinnean blàtha air mo ghruaidh
nuair a mhilleadh na ballan,
dol air birlinn mo nàmhaid
leis na ràmhan 's na sleaghan
air mo reic air son òir
gu ruig an tigh borbarra seo.

Feadan nam beann a' luathadh
birlinn nan lethcheud ràmh;
siùil gheala air an sìneadh
a' glàcadh osag an iar
gu taisdeal nan tonn gàireach.

Bu mhath leam coiseachd a rithisd
air a' mhachair uaine òirdheirc,
is fàinne geal an latha
gach maduinn ag éirigh.

S truagh nach robh sgiathan air mo dhruim
ga mo thoirt air ais gu tigh m'athar,
is gum bithinn a rithisd mar a bhà mi,
is mi òg a' dannsadh le aighearachd
dlùth do m' mhàthair aig banais
far na ghabh mi tlachd measg na h-òigridh
gùn sìoda orm 's obair-ghréis air,
's mo ghruaidh mar chaorainn a' làsadh
fo sgàil mo chùil bhuidhe dhualaich.

SLAVE WOMEN IN TAURIS

I will grieve along with you, o bird that sings a lament among the skerries of the sea; a song that is known to us who understand your never-ending call, o kingfisher.

I am like a wingless bird, far from the home of the Gael, bowed down under grief.

The drops warm on my cheeks when the walls were destroyed; going aboard the galley of my enemy with its oars and spears; sold for gold to this barbarous house.

Pipe of the mountains hastening the galley of fifty oars. White sails stretching, catching the western breeze to travel the sounding waves.

I would like to walk again on the splendid green machair, and the bright ring of the day arising each morning.

Would that I had wings on my back, to take me to my father's house, and I would be as I once was, young and dancing joyfully, close to my mother at a wedding, where I could be happy amongst the young people in my embroidered silk gown, and my cheek glowing like the rowan beneath the shade of my yellow braids.

MOLADH ARAINN

(bho sean Ghaidhlig *c.* 1100)

Arainn oirdheirc nan eildean uasal,
cuan a' bhualadh air do ghualainn,
eilean grinn anns am biadhar buidhnean
far an deargar na sleaghan liathghorm.

Os cionn a' chuan do bheanntan sìnte
lìonmhor na lùsan 'nad thorrach-chrìochan,
is greigheach treudach do raointean 's frìthean
's is coillteach sluaghach do roinnean sléibhteach.

Daimh dhonna fhiadhaich air do mheallan àrda
is dearcan-fhraoich air do mhòintean fàsail,
uisgeachan fionnar 'nad aibhnean gàireach
cnothan a' tuiteam à chraobhan-dàrach.

Is lìonmhor mialchon is gadhair-seilge
smeuran is airneig is droighneig meurach;
an iomall choille na tighean steidheil
is féidh air allaban fo bhilean geugach.

Air uachdar chreag gheibhear maise chorcuir,
feur gun lochd air do réidhlean gorma;
fasgadh seasgair fo dhìon a' mhonaidh
is bric a' leumadh air feadh nan lochan.

Is mìn do mhaghan 's is meith do mhucan
is leòir do chnòthan air mullach caltuinn,
meas nan craobh anns gach doire sìolmhor
birlinnean beartach fo sgàil do rudhan.

Eibhinn gach roinn dhiot nuair thig an samhradh
bidh eisg fo bhruaich gach uillt is aibhne;
bidh gairm nam faoileann fo stùcan geala
is caomh leinn daonnan an t-eilean Arainn.

IN PRAISE OF ARRAN

Splendid Arran of the noble hinds, the sea striking your shoulder, beautiful island where warrior bands are fed, where the blue-grey spears are reddened.

Your mountains stretched out above the sea, plentiful the herbs in your fruitful bounds, herds of cattle and horses in your meadows and forests, wooded and full of people your uplands.

The wild brown stag on your high eminences; blaeberries on your wild moors, cool waters in your rushing rivers, nuts falling from oak-trees.

Plentiful are greyhounds and hunting-dogs, blackberries and sloes and branching blackthorn. On the edge of woods are your well-found houses, and deer wandering under the branched trees.

On the surface of the rocks the bonnie lichen, grass without blemish on your greenswards; comfortable shelter in the protection of the moorland and trout leaping through each lochan.

Smooth are your plains, fat your swine, plentiful the nuts on the hazels. The fruit of the trees in each fertile wood, and rich galleons beneath your nesses.

Joyful each part of you when summer comes; there will be fish under the bank of each burn and river; the call of seagulls under your white cliffs. Beloved to us always, the isle of Arran.

NAUSICAA

"A ghruagaich òig an òr-fhuilt bhuidhe
co an duine tha 'nad dheoghaidh?
le coltas air mar mharaiche?"
"Fhuair mi esan air an tràigh!"

"C'àite an d'fhuair e 'n deise spaideil?
Cha bu shaor a leine geal . . ."
"Thug mi deise m'athair dha
is theid e dhachaidh leam gun dàil!"

"Phòsadh iomadh fear an eilein
nighean tocharach dhe do sheòrs';
nach feàrr leat duine comasach
seach seoladair a chaill a chùrs'?"

"Cha d' fhuair mi tairgse bhuapa fhathast;
cha bhi mi beò air fiughair a mhàin.
Carson a thilginn air àis
cothrom thanaig le muir-làn?"

NAUSICAA

"Young maiden of the yellow-gold hair
who is the man following you
who looks like a sailorman?"
"I found him on the shore!"

"Where did he get that smart suit?
His white shirt wasn't cheap . . ."
"I gave him my father's shirt,
and he'll be coming home with me right away."

"There's many a man of the island would marry
a tochered lass like yourself;
wouldn't you prefer a capable man
rather than a sailor that went off his course?"

"I haven't had an offer from them yet,
and I can't live on hope alone.
Why should I throw back
a chance that came in with the tide?"

EILEANAN

Thoir mo shòraidh gu Lanndaidh
eilean uaine Clann Domhnaill
crìdhe boidheadh Dal Riata
bidh thu daonnan 'nam chuimhne
bho Maol Odha gu Tràigh Ghruinneart
gus an tig mo la deireannach.

A Cholbhasa alainn
tha do machraichean samhach:
air do thraighean geal' aonaranach
bha mi sìtheil fo d' ghrian.
Ged nach b'unnam ach coigrich
air do laimrig bhig Scalasaig
dh'èirich m' inntinn is m'anam
nuair a chaidh mi air tìr ort.

A Mhuile nam mór-bheann
far an d'fhuair mi deagh fhialachd
ged nach b' fhada mo thadhal ort
cha dean mi do dhi-chuimhneachadh.
Eilean uasal Mhic 'illeathan
far an do rinn mi mo thriall-sa
bidh mi 'siùbhal nan sleibh ort
'h-uile la 'nam mhac-meanma.

Eileann Barraidh nam faoileann
eileag iomallach a' bhealaidh,
Eoligarraidh gu Cismaol
bithinn a' tadhal a rìthisd ort;
a' sealltuinn air Uibhist
's air a' Chuilfhionn ard Sgitheanach
nan robh thus a dhith oirnn
cha bhiodh Alba ann idir.

ISLANDS

Take my greeting to Islay
green isle of Clan Donald
lovely heart of Dalriada
you are aye in my memory,
Mull of Oa to Traighgruinneart
until my last day.

Beautiful Colonsay
your machairs are silent;
on your white lonely beaches
I was peaceful under the sun.
Though I was but a stranger
on your little pier at Scalasaig
my mind and my soul arose
when I went ashore on you.

O Mull of the high hills
where I got fine hospitality
though my visit to you was not long
I will not forget you;
noble island of Clan MacLean
where I made my journey
I will be travelling your moorlands
each day in my memory.

Isle of Barra of the seagulls
lonely isle of the broom,
Eoligarry to Kismul
I would be travelling you again;
looking on Uist
and the high Coolins of Skye,
if you were lacking to us
there would be no Scotland at all.

BEANNTAN AIR FAIRE

An uair a bhios an oidhche glan, soilleir
chi mi bho'n fhardach seo air Galldachd Lodainn
taobh thall an Abhainn Dubh, na beanntan àrda;
chi mi na Troisaichean mar barrabhallan air fàire,
am boidhchead gorma 'streapadh iarmailt an fheasgair.
Chan eil Gododdin an diugh ach mac-talla an inntinn sgoileir,
ach mur eil Somhairle no Eòin fhathast an Fionnlagan
tha Alba beò air traighean a' chuain siar.

Fo ghrian ordheirc an fheasgair tha m'inntinn a' gluasad;
bu mhiann leam eirigh mar Shuibhne an riochd eòin,
ach chan eil mi idir cho mallaichte no cho beannaichte ris-san;
chan eil geimhlean air m' aobrannan 'gam chumail an seo:
cuiridh mi am maireach m' aghaidh ris na beanntan ud
is a dheòin no a dh'aindheòin fagaidh mi Lodainn na mo dheidh.

Ach chan fhada nis gus am bi a' ghrian air dol fodha
is bheir an dorchadas dhomhsa leisgeul mo ghealtaireachd.

MOUNTAINS ON THE HORIZON

Whenever the evening is clear and bright, I can see from this
dwelling on the Lowlands of Lothian the high mountains on the
far side of Forth. I see the Trossachs like battlements on the
horizon, their blue beauty climbing the evening sky. Gododdin
today is but an echo in a scholar's mind, but if Somerled and
John are not in Finlagan, Alba still lives on the shore of the
western sea. My mind moves under the splendour of the
evening and I wish to rise like Suibhne in the form of a bird,
but I am neither so accursed nor so blessed as he. There are
no gyves on my ankles to keep me here. Tomorrow I will set my
face to those mountains and in spite of all leave Lothian behind
me. But it will not be long until the sun goes down, and darkness
will give me an excuse for my cowardice.

GEARAN FHILIDH

Righ, bha uair ann an Alba
is b'urrainn dhuinn each a chòsnadh
no is dòcha mart mur an robh gach duan slàn
ach theich na maithean 's dh'fhalbh iad
's ann an Lunainn a gheibh iad am bòsdadh,
's chan fhaigh aon fhilidh duais is fhiach a dhàn.

Cha dean sin *seòladh* no *comhad*
cha dean sinn *rann* no *lethrann*
cha ceangail sinn le *aicill* ciall ar duain;
an stuth a chuirear romhad
chan fhiach e fiù is lethbhonn
gun ghuth air paidhir bhròig dhe leadair bhuan.

Cha dean sinn *uaim* no *fioruaim*
chan dean sinn *dùnadh* le *saighidh,*
cha dean sinn *rannaigheacht bheag* no *dialtach mhór;*
claoidhte le sgornan tioram
cha dean sinn bàrdachd baigheil
mur eil fialachd aig gach filidh fial gu léoir.

A COMPLAINT OF POETS

Ree, there was a time in Scotland when we could earn a horse, or perhaps a cow if our verse was not up to scratch; but the nobles are fled and departed, they got their "boasting" in London, and no poet gets a reward that's worth his song. We make no "First-couplet" or "Second-couplet," we make no Verse or Half-verse, we do not tie the meaning of our song with *aicill*; the stuff which is put before you is not worth a half-sole, never mind a pair of good leather shoes. We do not make the alliteration internally, or alliteration at the end of lines, we do not end with the word we started with, we do not make great one-syllabled versification; overcome by a dry throat, we will make no joyful poetry unless each poet gets hospitality that is indeed hospitable.

47

THE GLEN O DRY BANES

Ae day the Twa-Sichtit cam doun the lang glen,
doun the lang glen o the deid dry banes . . .
the deid dry banes that were looms o men
nou liggin hauf-yirdit wi stour an stanes.

An a Voice cam duntin doun oot o the lift
oot o the lift that was toom an bare. . . .
"Wad ye gie the ward gin ye thocht ye'd shift
the hauses an harnpans ye've got doun there?"

"Gin ye thocht ye micht hansel thir bones wi thews
an hap aa thegither wi ticht new skin . . .
an claithe thir auld sinners in plaid an trews . . .
wad ye swall their breists wi a leevin win'! "

An the skreich o the seer on the birlin breeze
Stottit back frae the stany waa's o the glen:
"We hae muckle need o sic chiels as these . . .
thro the yetts o hell I wad cry thaim ben."

"Thir dreich dry banes here as pouthert as keel
an thir white harnpans that the glaivie split . . .
thir kists that were loused by the dirkies steel . . .
Gin ye grantit the pow'r I wad ettle at it."

"For ye ken we hae leevin banes eneuch
In bricht new skins happit roun wi claith . . .
but their spirits within are no sae teuch
as thir auld dry banes that want nocht but braith."

BROTHER DOVE

I, Colm, far from the snow-crested *sleibh*
in this calm and cloistered silence,
hear no longer the robber-haunted sea or the belling stag.
*Gigeste-si Dia linn ara fulsam ar fochidi.**

No terror of the Northmen by night,
only the quiet learning, the quiet writing,
here in Bobbio far from the dragon ships;
is oc precept sosceli atto.†

In a strange land, to strange tongues
we add our own to form a trinity:
Gaelic and Greek and Latin.
cia for-comam-ni riagoil sen-Grec hi sgribunt. . . .‡

The tongue of childhood
here in this sacred book
I now make blessed;
for the sake of *Isu mac De*§
Rex Iudaeorum,
Imperator Scottorum.

* You will pray to God with us that we may endure our tribulations.
† It is preaching the gospel that I am.
‡ though we preserve the ancient Greek rule in writing. . . .
§ Jesus son of God.

These are glosses from Continental MS Gospels, written 8th century.

IF MONDAY COMES . . .

Unwilling, with unsmiling Monday faces
the city's scholars enter Stalag School.
As fire drives bugs from wood
they swarm from Easterhouses, Glasshouses, Bleakhouses . . .
the bouldered Gobi of the week stretching before them.

The smirring rain feels dankly round my collar
as I range the playground with the other screws,
and just before Our Leader blows his whistle
across the street in a surviving tree
a city mavis mocks us with his song.

BRAXY

Below the runkled horns
out from a seething fleece
gouged sockets glared.
In the thick, drowning silence, hoodies rose
carrion-crop heavy, jeering in the grey glen.

Stepping from under the veil
I saw beyond Kintyre the comb of Arran;
Jura's giant breasts rose from the living earth,
Dunlossit's trees breathed on the silver Sound.

This corruption of the flesh,
this beauty beyond words
fuse in the mind to a unity
whose formula remains a secret.

NEW OFFICE BLOCK — EDINBURGH

In the mouth of the street
this ill-fitting denture
threatens to swallow us all;
trick house of cards:
take one, take one go on
don't tell me what it is
I know I know I know
better than you do pal.

Well-mannered stone
now elbowed rudely sideways
to accommodate mister this and mister that
and clerks and secretaries
and all their public relations.

TRON KIRK

Before they revised the universe
this steeple pointed unerringly to God;
a compass now gone wrong that merely blinds
important traffic at the city corner
or once a year becomes
the focal point of desperate saturnalia.

There is no echo of Knox in this crumbling sanctity;
broken the tenuous thread
that joined this cure of souls to Skellig Michael.

all polytheists now
who worship only the obvious
myriad manifestations of sterling worth.

In their symbols of integration
no mark of coming disintegration;
no prophet's cry can easily disturb
their useful, technical philosophies.

MR AND MRS ABSENTEE-LANDLORD

Darling . . . let's go to the Games this year . . .
For after all . . . you are the CHIEF . . .
And things in London are oh, so drear . . .
Better SOME glory, however brief . . .

I'm NOT the Chief dear, just the owner . . .
Though some of them may call me LAIRD . . .
(And other things!) I'm no condoner
Of poachers who would pull my beard.

But you look so NICE in a kilt, my love;
What do they call it? Ah! . . . philabeg . . .
Oh . . . those great long sticks with the hook above
And really you've got such a LOVELY LEG . . .
The Girls just SCREAM when they see you in it . . .
Sometimes I WISH I was a man . . .
I wouldn't wear trousers for a MINUTE . . .
I don't suppose a woman CAN?

Oh . . . it's all right for YOU, a WOMAN,
But I've never felt they really LIKE me . . .
I'm sure they think I'm not quite HUMAN . . .
And some of them (I KNOW) would SPIKE me
On those broadswords on the downstairs wall.
And that old WITCH, in the lower glen . . .
(I'm sure there's been bloodshed in her hall)
And the DRAINS . . . PLEASE let's not go AGAIN.

Well, REALLY dear, what ODD objections
I must say I think you're very funny . . .
Oh . . . they'll boast enough of their great connections
But there's none of them with any MONEY . . .
And you needn't worry at their complaining
And muttering in their GHASTLY lingo . . .
Heavens, last year when it was raining . . .
And you fixed up that tent for Bingo . . .
You'd think they'd show some GRATITUDE . . .
When they've nothing else to do but sing.
I really cannot stand their attitude . . .
And, oh . . . that awful CEILIDH THING
That just went on for hours and HOURS . . .
Song after song in that AWFUL gellick . . .
You'd really think dear that the Powers
That BE would rid us of that RELIC
Of the Dark Ages . . . Well, I don't know
If it's worth the trouble after all.
No, I don't think so. We'll *not* go!
We can always hold a Highland Ball
For the right people from the *City* . . .
At least they'll all know what to WEAR . . .
I always think it such a pity
Those MACS and things still LIVE up there.

Langshankit Edward's bitter banes
are happit nou in glory-stanes.
Man, hou his gruesome royal remains
wi mirth maun rattle
tae see the Bruce's prood domains
grazed by sic cattle.